# Early Childhood Units

## for

# Nursery Rhymes

*Written by Sandra Merrick*
*Edited by Karen Goldfluss*
*Illustrated by Cheryl Buhler, Sue Fullam,*
*Keith Vasconcelles and Theresa Wright*

**Teacher Created Materials, Inc.**
6421 Industry Way
Westminster, CA 92683
www.teachercreated.com
*©1992 Teacher Created Materials, Inc.*
Reprinted, 1999
Made in U.S.A.
**ISBN-1-55734-020-X**

# Table of Contents

# Introduction

The purpose of whole language is to teach children how to read. In *Whole Language Units for Nursery Rhymes* children learn to read using activities based on nursery rhymes. They also learn to enjoy and understand what they read. Students who are not ready to read will learn phonics, appreciate literature, hear rhyme and rhythm, acquire concepts, and understand language structure. Every effort has been made to involve thinking skills, so that children can analyze, classify, and create while learning to read.

Each unit in this book is organized to include some or all of the following activities:

- sample lesson plans
- center ideas
- flannel board patterns
- reproducible little books
- related literature
- creative writing
- sequencing
- word matching
- art projects
- phonics activities

Whether you choose to do some or all of the activities for each nursery rhyme, enjoy working on them with your class.

# What Is Whole Language?

In whole language, skills and activities are arranged around a literary experience. For example, children learn the sound of the letter 'p' after they study the nursery rhyme "Peter, Peter, Pumpkin Eater." The teacher emphasizes that learning the 'p' sound will help them learn to read words like pig and pear. Reading, language, writing, spelling, and speaking are not taught in separate units, but are related to a particular book, story, or poem.

Meaning is emphasized in whole language, but not by asking a few questions about the story. The class is immersed in meaning by repeated experiences with the story or poem. It is acceptable and desirable for students to memorize and act out the stories or poems.

In whole language, students usually use trade books or Big Books instead of traditional text books. If texts contain high quality selections, they can be used. Vocabulary is not introduced and defined before reading the story. The story is read first for enjoyment.

Creative writing is an important part of whole language. Children use ideas or patterns from the story to create new stories. Younger children will need lots of direction, modeling, and suggestions from the teacher.

Students use approximate or invented spelling during creative writing. Students are urged not to worry about correct spelling, but to sound out the word and spell it as accurately as they can. Older students can correct and edit a second draft.

In a whole language classroom, children are immersed in print. Walls and bulletin boards are covered with labeled pictures and creative writing. Copies of literature and Big Books are available in a reading corner. Copies of books "written" by the students are included.

# Presenting a Whole Language Unit

There are several ways of presenting whole language units. General suggestions are given below. Each nursery rhyme has its own sample lesson plan.

1. **Introduce the unit.** Activities that involve creative thinking skills are best. Examples of these include brainstorming, associating the new story with past experiences, and making predictions.

2. **Present the poem or story** using flannel board, magnetic board, chart, or Big Book activities. Make sentence strips for each poem and use them in a pocket chart when introducing or rereading a poem.

3. **Repeat the literature each day,** varying the method to maintain interest. Suggestions for rereading the poems are provided in the plans.

4. **Make a classroom book** for the children to read. A good size to use is ¼ of poster board. Copy the text of the story or poem using the patterns from this book, children's drawings, or enlarged little book pages.

5. **Copy the little books,** one for each child. Make a tape of the story or poem to use in a listening center. Students take the little books home to share with their parents.

6. **Use cloze sentences** (missing word) from the story to emphasize meaning and use of context clues. This is easy to do on an overhead by using an index card and covering a word.

7. **Make word rings.** Use 3" x 5" index cards, book rings, and a hole punch. Copy the selected word onto a card, punch a hole near the corner, and put the card onto the book ring. Add as many cards as you wish to create personalized word rings.

8. **Use the sample lessons.** Sample lessons are presented at the beginning of each unit. They provide across the curriculum suggestions and activities for several days, as well as a "Getting Ready" section for unit preparation. Adjust your choice of activities and daily scheduling to meet student needs. **Note:** A more extensive sample plan is presented in *Humpty Dumpty* in order to assist teachers in "getting started."

# Using the Patterns

For each of the stories or poems in this book, patterns of the characters and props are provided. Suggestions for making and using these patterns are provided below.

## Traditional Felt Figures

Trace the patterns onto felt squares, which can be purchased in craft, department, or fabric stores. Use very sharp scissors to cut. Attach pieces to each other using an extra heavy tacky craft or fabric glue. Include movable eyes (6mm size) and tiny pom pom noses (6 mm) if desired. Word cards to match the figures can be made from 1 ½" x 5" rectangles of heavy nonwoven smooth fabric interfacing. (Pellon 930® works well.) These will adhere easily to flannel boards. Then print the word with a fine point permanent marker. Use the felt figures and words to act out stories on the flannel board. Make two sets, one for the teacher and one for the children. Encourage children to make up their own stories using the figures.

## Quick Color-and-Cut Figures

Copy, color, and cut out the flannel board patterns in this book. Seek help from students, volunteer parents, and aides. Many copiers will copy on heavy stock, like index, tag, or construction paper. These papers can be purchased in many sizes, including the standard 8 ½" x 11". (Patterns can also be duplicated onto wallpaper samples cut to fit the copier. This eliminates coloring since only the features need to be highlighted with markers to make delightful, stuffed animal-like figures.) Laminate. Glue squares of felt to the back for flannel board use. Attach magnetic strips (available from craft stores) for use on magnetic boards.

## Figures for Overhead

Figures made from felt or paper can sometimes be used directly on the overhead if their outlines are distinct enough for easy identification. You may wish to use a copy machine or have a copy shop make overhead transparencies of the patterns and/or the Little Books. These can be colored with transparency pens, thus providing another way to use the patterns for storytelling and instructions.

# Using the Patterns *(cont.)*

## Fabric Interfacing Flannel Board Figures

Put heavy nonwoven interfacing over the patterns and trace with a permanent marker. Color with crayons. These can be ironed if they become wrinkled.

## Puppets and Paper Dolls

Give each child copies of the patterns to color, cut out, and glue to craft sticks for their own stick puppets. For a teacher set, copy the patterns onto heavy paper and laminate before taping to craft sticks. Place a set of the laminated, colored figures (without craft sticks) in a paper doll center for children's use. Encourage the children to make new clothes and accessories for the figures.

## Bulletin Boards

Enlarge the patterns to make related bulletin boards. Use an opaque projector if you wish to make large pieces. Otherwise you may wish to simply enlarge on a copy machine.

## To Make a Big Book

Make a Big Book to present the story, or for the children to read in centers (a good size to use is ¼ of a large poster board). Copy the text of the story or poem, writing a few lines on each page. Draw pictures of the story or poem on each page. As an alternative, use a copy machine to enlarge patterns from this book; cut, color, and glue patterns to the pages. Or, have the children illustrate the pages.

## To Assemble Little Books

Have copies of the Little Book pages made for each child. Cut along the dotted lines. During class have the students color the pages. Show them how to put the pages in order. Staple completed books. Keep the little books at school for a few days while you do some of the suggested activities with them. Then let children bring them home to share.

## Art Projects

You can also use the flannel board patterns for art projects. Make copies and glue them onto stiff paper. Students may trace, color, cut, and glue them to create their own pictures. Place art supplies on a cart or in a central location of the room.

# Using the Phonics Pages

Each unit has a related phonics page to be used as an activity sheet and/or clothespin game.

Reproduce the phonics pages that you plan to use as center games onto index paper. If a more durable paper is desired, glue a copy of the game to poster or tag board. Laminate, if possible. File folders work well, too. Experiment with colored paper or index to eliminate the need for coloring. As an alternative, ask older student volunteers or teacher aides to color the pictures. For small groups, or when using phonics games at centers, make several copies of each game.

The phonics pages in each unit may be used in a variety of ways.

**Worksheet:** Duplicate a copy for each child. Direct students to color all of the pictures that begin with the sound of the letter on the page. This is a good evaluation tool for checking phonics knowledge.

**Clothespin Game:** Duplicate, color, and laminate the phonics pages. Have students clip a clothespin to each picture that begins with the sound of the letter on the page. These can be placed in a center.

**Variation:** Instead of using clothespins, have students mark choices with markers such as beans, seeds, or plastic disks.

# Using Word Banks

A word bank is a collection of related words. It should grow and be added to as children learn more about the topic being studied. Children have a sense of ownership in the word bank as they contribute to the list. This is a quick, fun way for students to integrate reading and writing.

Word banks may be used in conjunction with word rings (see page 4). When given the choice of words to put on their word rings, students are likely to choose those from the word bank. A display of flannel board patterns depicting a poem that has just been read will also influence a student's choice of words to add to the word rings.

Word banks should be prominently placed in the classroom. Be sure words are large enough to be visible from different areas of the room. Display words on colorful backgrounds, using an appropriate theme. For example, a word bank for "Rain, Rain" could be attached to a large umbrella made and decorated from butcher paper. Or, words could be written in raindrop shapes falling around an umbrella entitled "Rain, Rain, Go Away."

# Extending into Centers

Classroom centers provide games and activities that are as important as shared reading. They are high interest learning areas for group or individual endeavors.

**Reading Center with Flannel Board:** Put a flannel board or magnetic board in a center. Make an additional set of pattern figures from each nursery rhyme for the children to use in the center. Set out patterns and corresponding 1 ½" x 5" nonwoven interfacing word cards (page 5) from the nursery rhyme you are reading for the children to match with the flannel board figures.

This center should be cozy, comfortable and accessible. Include bean bag chairs or large pillows. Provide a large variety of nursery rhyme books and related literature. Have books on different reading levels and include picture books and wordless books. Don't forget to display student-authored books.

**Listening Center:** Use a blank tape and record your own version of each nursery rhyme. Provide headphones and a tape recorder and have students follow along in the unit Little Books as they listen to the tapes. Children enjoy making their own recordings. Have them retell the story in their own words, using the little book illustrations as a guide.

**Block Center:** Provide blocks of various shapes and sizes. Encourage students to use them to build structures appropriate to some of the nursery rhymes. Use the patterns to make poster board or laminated tagboard figures. Students can use patterns as paper dolls for dramatic play in the center.

**Math Center:** Make felt figures for the children to use as manipulatives. Encourage them to create patterns with the figures, to make up story word problems, and to use them for simple addition and subtraction problems.

**Science Center:** Provide materials and displays for children to manipulate. For example, have water activities ready for "Fish Alive," "Jack and Jill," and "Rain, Rain." A variety of egg projects for "Humpty Dumpty" and planting activities for "Mary, Mary, Quite Contrary" or "Peter, Peter, Pumpkin Eater" could be added to the center.

# Sample Lessons for "Humpty Dumpty"

## Getting Ready

Make a chart of "Humpty Dumpty" to display. See Little Book (pages 19-21) for text. Use patterns (pages 13 and 14) to decorate.

Make sets of Humpty Dumpty flannel board figures (pages 13-14) for presenting the poem and for the children to have at the centers. Prepare sets of word cards with the words: Humpty; Dumpty; fall; wall; horses; men; egg; a; king; king's; sat. Make a set of felt or construction paper letters for matching beginning letters to words. Provide nursery rhyme cassette tapes for listening centers and blocks for wall building in the block center. Set up the Phonics Activity using directions on page 7.

## Day 1

**Before reading** "Humpty Dumpty," display the flannel board figure, a model of Humpty Dumpty (if available), and some eggs. Ask the following questions: Does anyone know who this is? Is he real or make-believe? Where do real eggs come from? What usually happens to them?

**Introduce** the nursery rhyme. Use the flannel board to present "Humpty Dumpty" the first time. Read the poem a second time, and ask the children to join in. Some students may want to recite the poem while the teacher puts the figures on the flannel board. If you have a cassette recorder, tape and sing the nursery rhyme.

**Draw a Humpty Dumpty egg.** Distribute copies of page 18. Have children trace the oval shape with their fingers several times. Those who are able may wish to write "egg" or "This is an egg." Others may choose to simply write 'e.' Allow students to color in the egg shape and add features.

**Practice sequencing** by making copies of each page of the Little Book on tagboard or index paper. (Be sure to delete page numbers first.) Glue them onto felt (for flannel board), or back with magnetic strips (for magnetic board). Have students practice putting the pages in order.

## Day 2

**Reread "Humpty Dumpty"** using a large chart or a big book. Ask students: Who fell? Off of what did he fall? What was he doing there? What happened to Humpty Dumpty?

**Dramatize** "Humpty Dumpty." A stuffed Humpty Dumpty doll can easily be made by cutting two pieces of fabric in large egg shapes, stuffing with cotton, and sewing around the sides. Add features with permanent marking pens. Have the class recite the poem while a child holds the doll and pushes him off a chair when Humpty has "a great fall." Children on brooms or stick horses can be the king's men.

# Sample Lessons for "Humpty Dumpty" *(cont.)*

**Introduce beginning sound 'h.'** Place the Humpty and horse flannel board figures on the overhead. Display and discuss pictures of words that begin with 'h.' Brainstorm other 'h' words. Where appropriate, use the flannel board patterns along with lower case beginning letters for each pattern. Review the beginning sounds. Locate the words on the chart, Big Book, or word bank. Felt letters can be rolled up and placed in egg-shaped hosiery containers. Pass out the "eggs" to students. Let them come up and match their letter to the correct flannel board pattern. Some students may be able to match word cards to patterns.

**Follow up** by reading *Are You My Mother?* by P. D. Eastman (Random, 1960). Remind children that Humpty Dumpty was shaped like an egg. In this related literature, a baby bird tries to find its mother. After reading the book, make up a poem about the day Humpty the Bird hatched. Record it on a chart and illustrate.

Example:

*The Humpty Bird*

*Sat on a wall.*

*He flew away,*

*And did not fall.*

## Day 3

**Reread "Humpty Dumpty"** using an overhead projector. Copy the Little Book pages onto transparency sheets. Ask students to recite the rhyme together and try to match some of the words to those in the word bank, on word cards, etc.

**Do egg math** using felt eggs for counting, adding, subtracting, and matching numerals to sets of eggs. Make up stories about how many eggs hatched and how many did not. Follow the same procedure using rocks or beans in egg cartons.

**Match words.** Print words from the word card list (page 9, Getting Ready) onto 3" x 5" index cards and distribute them to students. Match the index card words to the word cards prepared from interfacing. Some students may be able to match words to flannel board figures or read sentence strips and match them to figures or poem scenes.

**Prepare the Little Book** on pages 19-21. This may be done ahead of time or students may assemble them in class. Have children try to match some of the word cards with the text of the Little Book. Call out other words and see if the students can locate them. Give hints if necessary. Let the students color their booklets.

# Sample Lessons for "Humpty Dumpty" *(cont.)*

## Day 4

**Reread** "Humpty Dumpty" with students following along in their Little Books.

**Introduce the Phonics Activity** on page 17 as a clothespin game. (See page 7 for directions on using the phonics pages.)

**Make word rings.** Use some of the cards from the word card lesson. Work with a small group of students while others play in centers. Read the poem again and ask the children which words they would like to learn to read. Punch a hole in each card and place on an individual word ring for each child. Add more words on following days. Students keep word rings in their desks to practice reading and writing.

**Learn about eggs.** Remind children that Humpty Dumpty was shaped like an egg. (Introduce the term "oval.") Ask what kinds of animals lay eggs? Then read *Chickens Aren't the Only Ones* by Ruth Heller (Putnam, 1981). If available, display and label pictures of some of the animals mentioned in the story.

**Discover what is inside an egg.** Bring in raw eggs and have students break them apart on paper plates (demonstrate this first). Discuss the parts of the egg. Notice how it feels, smells, and looks.

As an extension, prepare a scrambled egg breakfast in class.

## Day 5

**Reread** "Humpty Dumpty" using lines from the poem written on overhead transparencies. Cover a word in a sentence (cloze) and ask students to identify the missing word. Display a transparency of the entire poem and have the class follow along in choral reading.

As an alternative, make sentence strips for each line of the poem and use them in a pocket chart. Create poems with the class using the first two lines only and changing the ending. For example: *Humpty Dumpty sat on a rock; Humpty Dumpty lost his red sock.* These could be displayed and illustrated or made into a Big Book. Or, write the new poem on sentence strips for use in a pocket chart. Children join in choral reading. Some students may want to choose sentence strips to read to the class.

# Sample Lessons for "Humpty Dumpty" *(cont.)*

**Put all of your eggs in one basket** with an egg toss. Bring in plastic eggs and a few large baskets (laundry baskets work well). Divide the class into groups and have them practice egg tossing.

**Write "If I Were Humpty" stories** using student dictated ideas. Have the class bring in photographs of themselves. Distribute egg patterns (page 18) and decorate them with lots of color. Cut out the egg. Have each student add the photo to the center of the egg and glue it to a piece of construction paper. Copy each student's ideas into a story on the back of the paper. Hang the stories on a wire or from the ceiling, or make them into a class book.

**Match pictures to words.** Copy several sets of Egg Match-ups from pages 15-16 onto heavy index paper. Cut around the egg shapes and along the lines, separating the words from the pictures. Place sets into manila envelopes for use at the reading center.

**Put puzzles "together again."** Discuss why it would have been difficult to put Humpty back together again. Have several age-appropriate puzzles available for students to use at a center. Students can work independently or in small groups to complete puzzles.

**Read** *Horton Hatches the Egg* by Dr. Seuss (Random, 1940). Discuss the following: How was Horton faithful? What do the words, "He meant what he said and he said what he meant," tell you? Can elephants lay eggs? Is this a real or make believe story? (Compare it to *Chickens Aren't the Only Ones*.)

# Patterns

# Patterns *(cont.)*

# Egg Match-ups

See page 12 for directions.

**Humpty**

**fall**

**egg**

**horse**

# Egg Match-ups (cont.)

See page 12 for directions.

wall

men

king

sat

# Phonics Activity

See page 7 for directions.

17 *#020 Whole Language Units for Nursery Rhymes*

# Egg Pattern

See activities on pages 9 and 12.

18

# Little Book

My Little Book of
# "Humpty Dumpty"

Name _____

## Humpty Dumpty sat on a wall,

1

# Little Book (cont.)

## Humpty Dumpty had a great fall;

2

## All the King's horses

3

# Little Book *(cont.)*

## And all the King's men

4

## Couldn't put Humpty together again.

5

# Sample Lessons for "Rain, Rain"

## Getting Ready

Make a chart of "Rain, Rain" to display. See Little Book (pages 30-31) for text. Use some of the illustrations from the unit to decorate the chart.

Prepare a simplified weather calendar for the classroom (see page 26). Set up an outdoor thermometer and wind sock, if possible. Include a weather report in the morning calendar activities. Arrange morning weather walks and follow up with weather related questions.

Stock the reading center with fiction and nonfiction books about weather. Provide enough blocks (large cardboard blocks or shoe boxes work well) to build shelters from the rain. In the listening center, have cassette recordings about weather and weather sounds. Make extra flannel board figures and interfacing word cards for students. Display a word bank as on page 7. Add words as needed.

## Day 1

**Present the poem using pictures of rain scenes.** Ask children what they like and dislike about rain. Where does rain come from? What is thunder? What do people need on a rainy day? Read "Rain, Rain."

**Make Johnny the Weather Boy** using the patterns on pages 24-25. Dress him appropriately as part of the daily calendar activities.

**Read and dramatize** "Ducks in the Rain" from *Read-Aloud Rhymes for the Very Young* selected by Jack Prelutsky (Alfred A. Knopf, 1986).

## Day 2

**Reread the poem using transparencies** of the Little Book (pages 30-31). Sing "Rain, Rain" with the class several times, substituting student names for Johnny.

**Write new poems.** Decide what Johnny would say if he were a frog or a duck. Then write, display, and illustrate a class poem.

For example:    *Rain, rain, come and stay.*

*In the rain we like to play.*

**Read *Rain*** by Robert Kalan (Greenwillow Books, 1978). The illustrations and text are sure to encourage discussion about where rain comes from, where it falls, and what a rainbow is.

**Create a rainbow** by placing a prism in front of a light source. Follow up with rainbow drawings, using crayons or watercolors. (Provide pre-drawn rainbow outlines if necessary.)

# Sample Lessons for "Rain, Rain" *(cont.)*

## Day 3

**Reread "Rain, Rain."** Use the large chart to recite it with children. Have students choose word cards from the poem to use on word rings. Find objects from the classroom that begin with 'r.' Label them.

**Make cloud pictures** by gluing cotton balls on light blue construction paper. Add drawings or paintings of children playing.

**Prepare the Little Book** (pages 30-31), following directions on page 6. Have students color the pages and keep them in class for a few days.

**Observe the wonders of water** through science and literature. Read *Rain Drop Splash* by Alvin Tresselt (Lothrop, 1946) or *Time of Wonder* by Robert McCloskey (Penguin, 1957). Follow up by observing the ripples made by dropping pebbles in pans of water. Make a puddle picture. Give each child a sticky dot to put in the center of a paper. Have them draw larger and larger circles around it for a bulls-eye effect. Color like a rainbow.

## Day 4

**Reread "Rain, Rain"** while students follow along in their Little Books. Some may wish to recite the pages to the class. Sing "It's Raining, It's Pouring" and add motions to the lyrics.

**Solve the riddles.** Display, read, and discuss the following riddles:

*From the clouds,*
*Down, down, down,*
*On the ground,*
*We dance around.*
*What are we?* **(raindrops)**

*I see the lightning flash.*
*I hear the thunder loud.*
*When rain comes down,*
*I hide behind a cloud.*
*Who am I?* **(sun)**

**Enjoy a phonics snack.** Read *Cloudy With a Chance of Meatballs* by Judi Barrett (Macmillan, 1978). At snack time ask students to name foods that begin with 'r.' Then hand out and enjoy raisins. Do the phonics activity on page 29, using raisin markers to identify 'r' words.

**Make the Itty Bitty Rain Book.** Copy student pages 27 and 28 back to back. Cut along the dotted line and lay little pages 3 and 4 on top of little pages 1 and 6. Fold along the solid lines and staple the book. Have children color the pages. Read the words and develop a class story by following the sequenced pictures.

# Patterns

For use on the flannel board, make a copy of the Weather Boy from felt; cut out, and add features. Then make copies of the other patterns; cut out without tabs, and glue to felt. Use patterns to dress the Weather Boy.

For use as a paper doll, make a copy for each child. Cut out Weather Boy and clothes. Use tabs to attach the clothing.

# Patterns *(cont.)*

*Rain, Rain*

# Weather Calendar

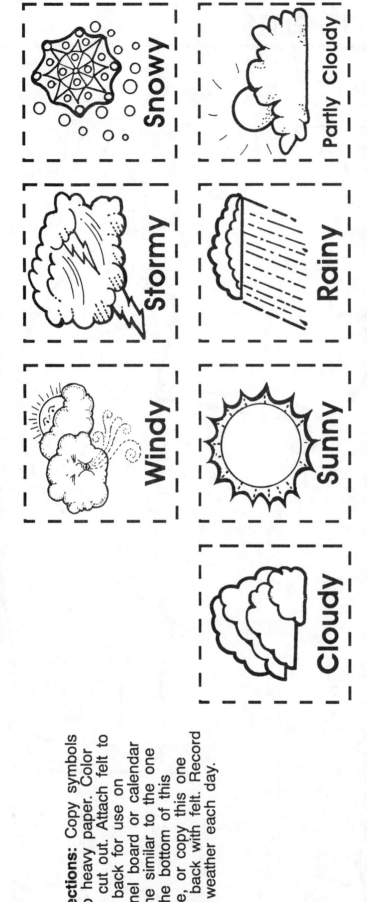

**Snowy**

**Partly Cloudy**

**Stormy**

**Rainy**

**Windy**

**Sunny**

**Cloudy**

**Directions:** Copy symbols onto heavy paper. Color and cut out. Attach felt to the back for use on flannel board or calendar frame similar to the one at the bottom of this page, or copy this one and back with felt. Record the weather each day.

| Monday | Tuesday | Wednesday | Thursday | Friday |
|--------|---------|-----------|----------|--------|
|        |         |           |          |        |

See directions on page 23.

The
End

My
Itty
Bitty
Rain
Book

Name_____

rain

5

cloud

2

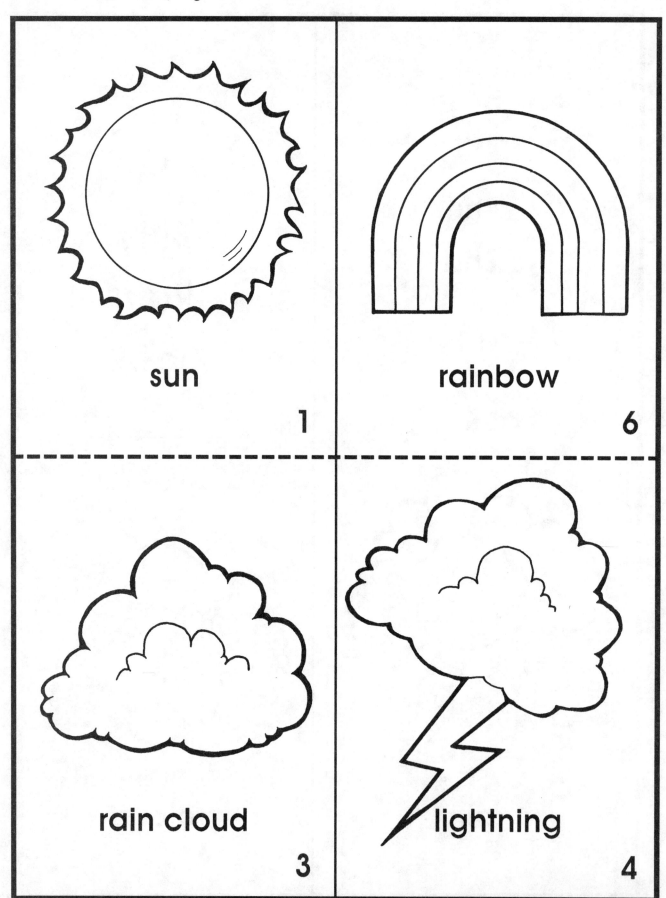

sun

1

rainbow

6

rain cloud

3

lightning

4

# Phonics Activity

See directions on page 23.

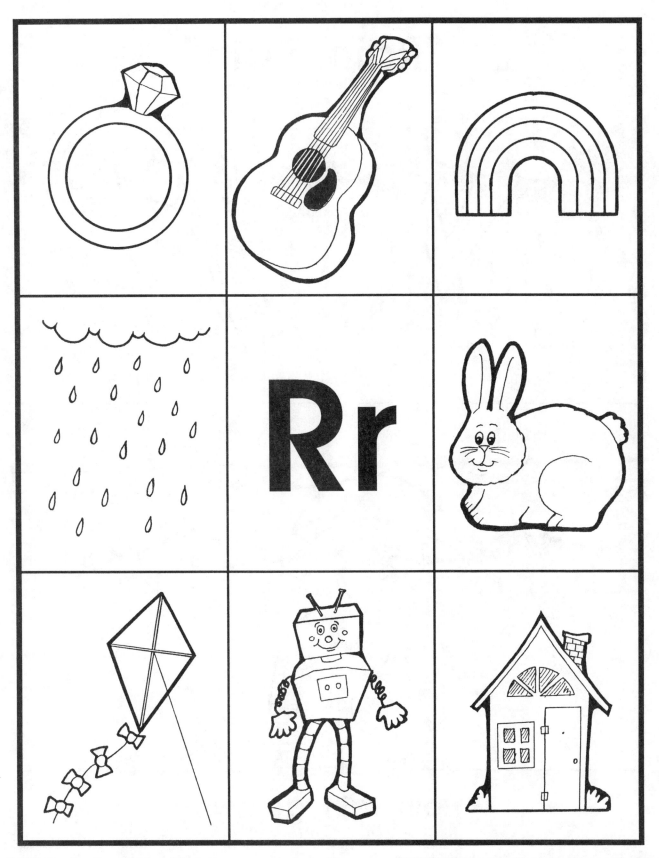

# Little Book

## My Little Book of
# "Rain, Rain"

Name _____

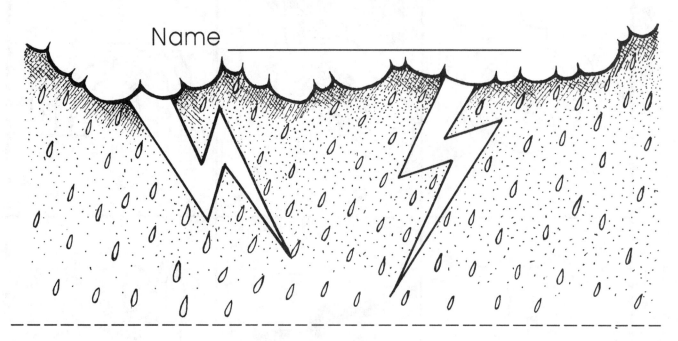

## Rain, rain, go away,

1

# Little Book (cont.)

## Come again another day.

2

## Little Johnny wants to play.

3

# Sample Lessons for "Fish Alive"

## Getting Ready

Prepare a big book using the poem "Fish Alive." See Little Book (pages 40-42) for text. Use the fish from the pattern pages or Little Book pages. Make flannel board pieces from the pattern pages and write a numeral on each fish, using a permanent marker. Make felt hands with numbered fingers for counting. Have science and art materials available, prepare phonics game (page 39), and set up reading, listening, and science centers (see page 8 for suggestions).

## Day 1

**Introduce "Fish Alive"** by bringing in fish to observe and to spark discussion. Or, display large, colorful pictures of fish. Ask students what they already know about fish, if they have ever been fishing, and how fish are different from people. Display ten fish on the overhead, flannel board, or wall to use while reading the poem to the class. Ask questions about the poem.

**Make fish bracelets**. Work with small groups to make bracelets for the *right* hand. Have students use the small fish pattern on page 34 to trace and draw six fish. Punch a hole in each fish, as shown, and write 1, 2, 3, 4, 5 on the fish. Label the sixth fish with the word "fish." Tie fish on yarn to make a bracelet for each child. Have children wear their bracelets on their right wrists to learn left and right, counting, and the word "fish."

**Practice the letter and sound of 'f.'** Collect a group of items that begin with 'f' and a group that do not. Ask children to identify the objects and determine if the beginning letter is 'f.' Distribute objects to students. Have those with objects beginning with 'f' move to one side of the room while those whose objects do not begin with 'f' go to the opposite side. Switch objects and repeat. Identify other 'f' objects in the room.

## Day 2

**Reread "Fish Alive."** Prepare ten pieces of construction paper with fish shapes on each. On the first, glue one fish, on the second, two, and so on. Distribute these to ten students. Hang pages around each child's neck by punching two holes at the top of each paper and attaching yarn. Read the poem and have students stand up and display their fish at the appropriate time. Use these pages for future counting activities.

Display the following riddle and ask students to guess what it is:

*I like to eat*
*Worms and bugs.*
*I just get hooks.*
*I never get hugs.*
*What am I? (**fish**)*

Make up a riddle board with other fish riddles and illustrations.

# Sample Lessons for "Fish Alive" *(cont.)*

**Practice sorting**. Be sure children have had prior experience with sorting. (Unifix cubes®, buttons, pegs, etc.) Use the patterns on pages 35-37 to do a flannel board sorting activity. Make felt fish of two different colors. Glue on wiggly eyes or make eyes with a permanent marker. Tie a piece of yarn around the flannel board to divide it into two sections. Working in small groups, have students sort the fish first by color and then by size.

**Make Little Books** using pages 40-42. Have students color these and bring them home after they have been used for class activities.

## Day 3

**Reread "Fish Alive."** Have children pantomime the actions and finger count as the poem is being read from a transparency, chart, or Big Book.

**Use a phonics clothespin game** to reinforce the letter 'f.' Prepare phonics page 39 as suggested on page 7. Have students clip the clothespins onto the pictures which begin with 'f.'

**Make fish necklaces**. Copy and cut out the large fish pattern (page 34) onto colored index paper. Punch a hole near the mouth and attach yarn for a necklace. Have each student name 3 or 4 items that begin with 'f'and write them on the fish.

**Prepare a science center for Sink or Float experiments** (page 38). Place the following items in a plastic basket at the center for the children to use: craft stick, large nail, fishing cork, large rock, penny, plastic fork, plastic lid, toy boat, small plastic bottle (tightly sealed), piece of sponge. Provide containers with water and have students test whether objects sink or float. Using the activity sheet on page 38, ask students to circle items that sink.

## Day 4

**Reread "Fish Alive"** while the children follow along in their Little Books. Invite those who can to recite the poem for the class.

**Prepare a magnetic fishing game.** Make two fishing poles by attaching small magnets to one end of pieces of yarn and tying the other ends of the yarn to sticks or dowels. Use the pattern on page 34 to make ten fish on colored index cards. Put gummed coding dots on each fish: one on the first; two on the next, and so on. Laminate. Attach a paper clip on the mouth of each fish. Have children take turns catching fish and placing them in correct numerical order on the floor. Students can catch fish with words on them. They must say the word in order to keep the fish.

**Learn facts about fish** by reading and discussing *What Is a Fish?* by David Eastman (Troll, 1982) or *First Look at Fish* by Millicent E. Selsam and Joyce Hunt (Walker, 1972).

# Patterns

See pages 32-33 for suggested activities.

NOTE: Use small fish for magnetic fishing game. Large fish can also be used while reading "Fish Alive." Make fish necklaces as on page 33. Give each student a fish with a number from 1-10 on it. Have students stand up when their numbers are called.

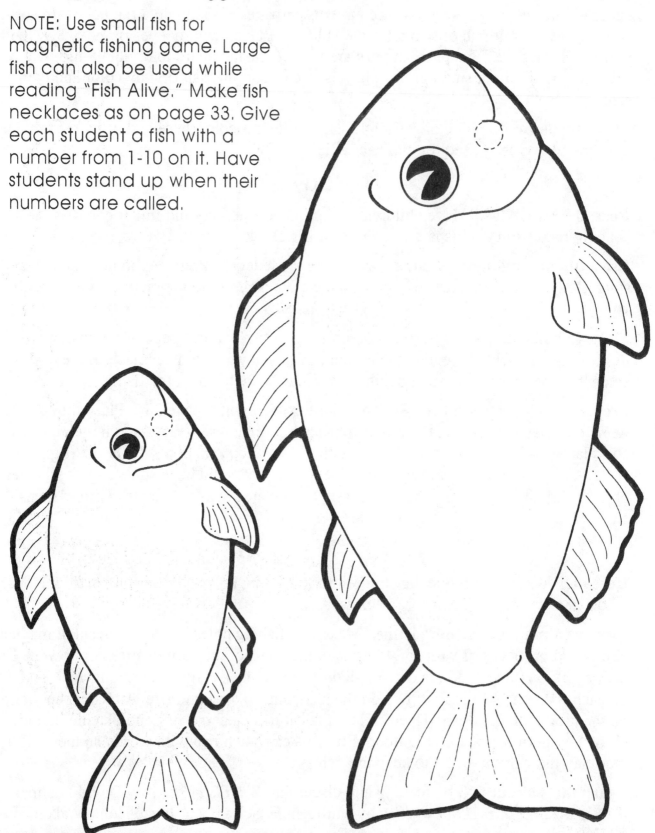

34

# Patterns *(cont.)*

See page 33 for suggested activities.

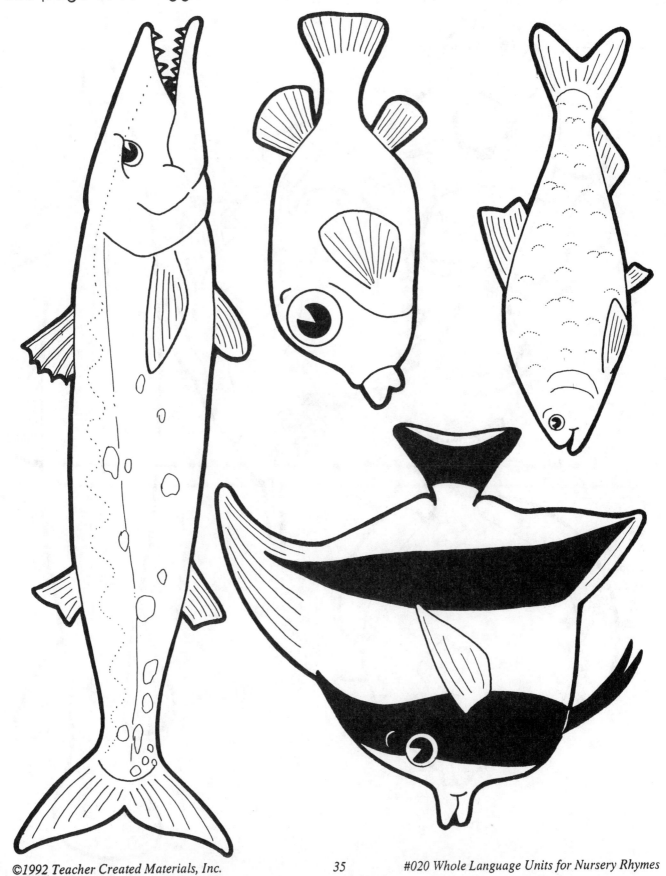

# Patterns *(cont.)*

See page 33 for suggested activities.

# Patterns *(cont.)*

See page 33 for suggested activities.

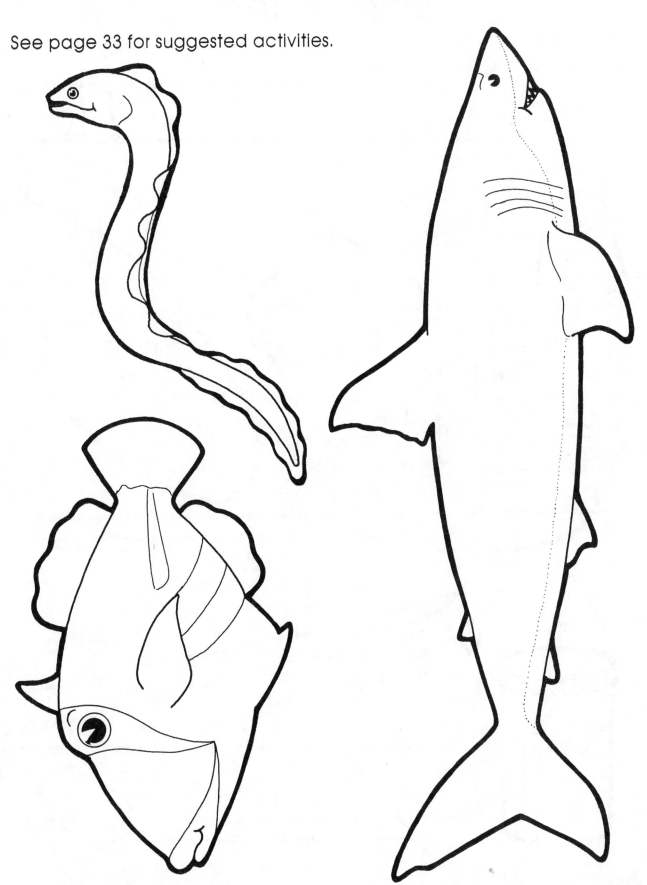

Name _____

# Sink or Float

**Directions:** Circle the things that sink.

# Phonics Activity

See page 33 for suggested activity.

# Little Book

My Little Book of

# "Fish Alive"

Name _____

1 2 3 4 5

## I caught a fish alive.

1

# Little Book *(cont.)*

2

## I let him go again.

3

# Little Book (cont.)

## Why did you let him go?
## Because he bit my finger so.

4

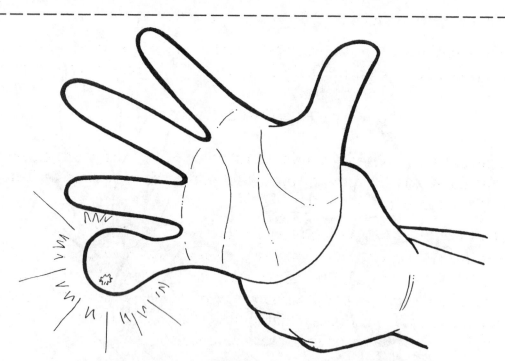

## Which finger did he bite?
## The little one, on the right.

5

# Sample Lessons for
# "Peter, Peter, Pumpkin Eater"

## Getting Ready

Prepare a pumpkin patch bulletin board with a large pumpkin shape in the center. Write the poem inside. See Little Book (pages 49-51) for text. Have vines and smaller pumpkins (1 per student) surrounding it. Put student photographs and names in each pumpkin. (Allow room for other writing as well.)

## Day 1

**Introduce the poem** by discussing the bulletin board. Talk about what pumpkins are, where they come from, and pumpkin foods. Read "Peter, Peter, Pumpkin Eater" from the bulletin board. Ask students what they think it would be like to live in a pumpkin and if they would like it.

**Practice pumpkin seed math.** Distribute pumpkin seeds for counting and estimation activities. Match seeds to other manipulatives, such as Unifix cubes®, for set-to-set correspondence. Make posters representing the numbers 1-10 by gluing seeds to construction paper. (For example, write the number 5; then glue and circle a group of 5 seeds.) Displayed posters can be used for counting practice.

**Set up a word bank** inside a pumpkin shape, or make vines from thick green yarn and attach words printed on green leaves to it. Children may use these to start word rings.

## Day 2

**Reread the poem** using overhead transparencies of the Little Book on pages 49-51. Ask children to find the words "Peter" and "pumpkin," and the rhyming words, "Peter/eater" and "shell/well" in the text.

**Display pictures of fruits and vegetables.** Decide in which category each belongs. Discuss why fruits and vegetables are important to our diets. Have children cut out small pictures of fruits and vegetables from magazines or seed catalogs. Label and glue them onto 4" x 6" index cards (laminate, if possible) and place them in the reading or science center for children to sort. Add books about food. Ask students to name favorite foods. Write student responses on their bulletin board pumpkins.

**Distribute and assemble the Little Book** of the nursery rhyme (pages 49-51). Color the pictures and read the poem together.

# Sample Lessons for "Peter, Peter, Pumpkin Eater" *(cont.)*

## Day 3

**Reread "Peter, Peter, Pumpkin Eater"** using flannel board figures. Sing the poem to the tune of "Twinkle, Twinkle."

**Extend the concept of unusual houses.** Read *Ottie Slockett* by Ida Luttrell (Dial, 1990) and talk about what it would be like to live in a shoe, a pumpkin, etc. Display and compare pictures of real houses around the world. Discuss and show book illustrations of various animal homes.

**Build unusual homes in the block center.** Allow students to look at home magazines and cut out pictures of different kinds of houses. Place them on a wall near the block center. Encourage children to build unusual houses and/or the kind of house in which they would like to live.

## Day 4

**Read "The Further Adventures of Peter's Wife"** using a transparency of page 46. Reproduce copies of the patterns from page 45 onto index weight paper. Have children cut out the patterns and glue them onto craft sticks for puppets. Prepare several simple pumpkin, apple, flower, and shoe patterns from tagboard. (Make them large enough for Peter and his wife to fit in.) Cut a door in each and have children use the stick puppets to dramatize the poem. Keep these in a center.

**Practice sequencing.** Ask students to use the stick puppets and apple, flower, pumpkin, and shoe houses to retell "The Further Adventures of Peter's Wife" in sequential order.

**Review the letter 'p'** using word banks, poems, and labeled classroom objects. Have students color in the pictures that begin with 'p' on phonics page 48.

**Help Peter find his wife.** Ask children to trace the paths in the maze on page 47 to find the one that leads to Peter's wife. They may use crayons, pencils, or fingers.

**"The Further Adventures of Peter's Wife"**

Peter's wife did not like living in a pumpkin,

So she went to live in an apple.

There was a worm in the apple,

So she went to live in a flower.

There was a bee in the flower,

So she went to live in the Old Woman's shoe.

There were too many children in the shoe,

So she went back to live in the pumpkin,

And she liked it very well.

# Patterns

See activity suggestions on page 44.

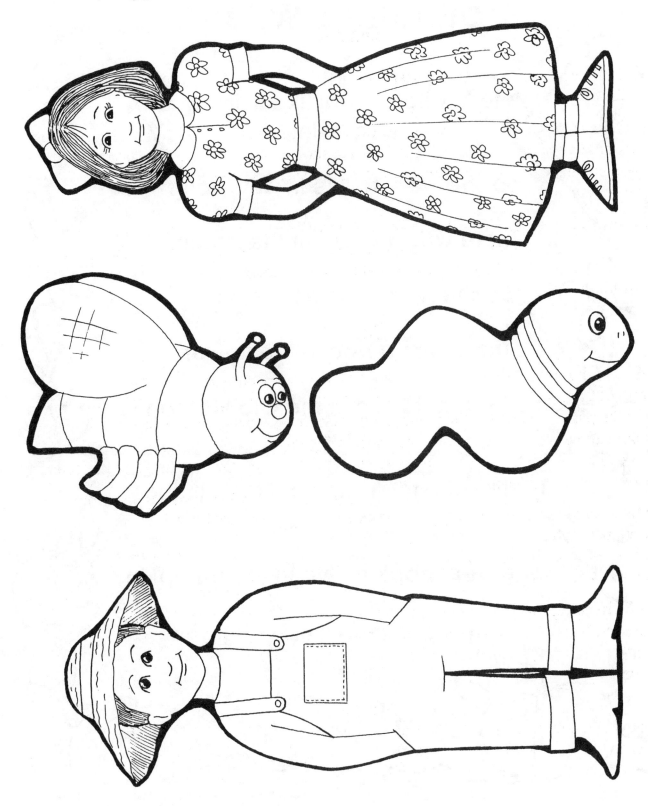

# "The Further Adventures of Peter's Wife"

Peter's wife did not like living in a pumpkin,

So she went to live in an apple.

There was a worm in the apple,

So she went to live in a flower.

There was a bee in the flower,

So she went to live in the Old Woman's shoe.

There were too many children in the shoe,

So she went back to live in the pumpkin,

And she liked it very well.

# Help Peter Find His Wife

**Directions:** Find the one correct path to Peter's wife.

#020 Whole Language Units for Nursery Rhymes

*Peter, Peter, Pumpkin Eater*

# Phonics Activity

See page 44 for suggested activity.

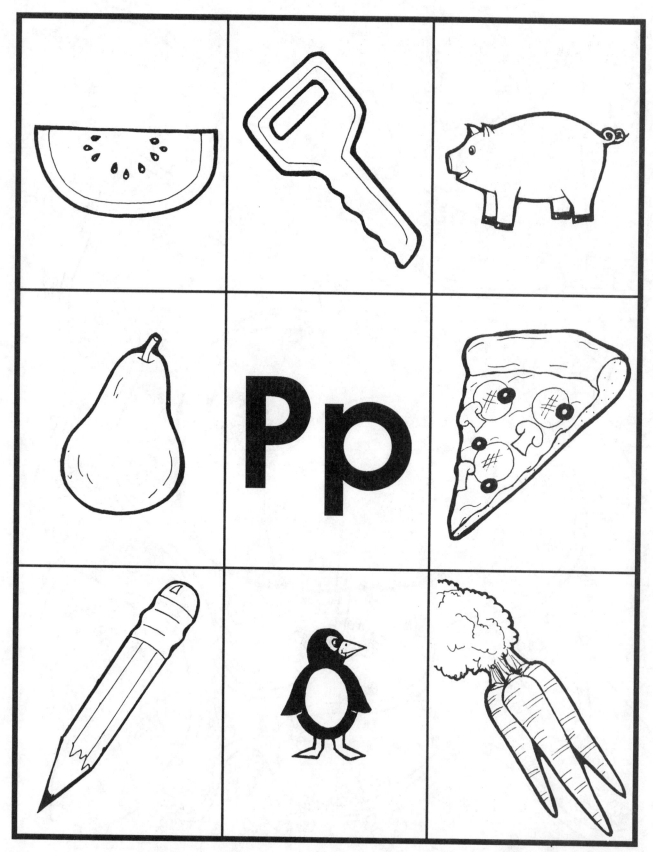

# Little Book

My Little Book of

# "Peter, Peter, Pumpkin Eater"

Name _____

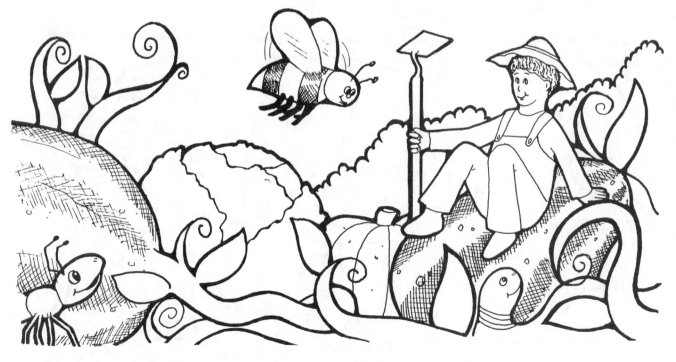

## Peter, Peter, Pumpkin Eater,

1

# Little Book (cont.)

## Had a wife and couldn't keep her;

2

## He put her in a pumpkin shell

3

# Little Book *(cont.)*

## And there he kept her very well.

4

# The End

5

# Sample Lessons for "Mary, Mary, Quite Contrary"

## Getting Ready

Prepare a science center for seed planting. Display pictures of flowers and plants. Place magazines and books in the reading center and nursery rhyme and related literature tapes in the listening center. Make copies of flannel board and/or index paper patterns (from pages 54-55) for centers. Make a word bank with large sunflower shapes. Add words to petals. Label the word bank "Our Word Garden."

## Day 1

**Find out what children already know about plants.** Bring in plants of various kinds and talk about types of gardens. Brainstorm what plants need to grow. Display pictures of plants and flowers and ask children to name some. Discuss size, color, similarities, and differences between them. Go for a walk and observe plants.

**Present "Mary, Mary, Quite Contrary"** using a Big Book, chart, or flannel board patterns. See Little Book (pages 59-61) for text. Discuss the meaning of contrary. Ask what might have made Mary contrary. Talk about feelings and how facial expressions can reflect emotions. Have children draw four circles and illustrate facial expressions for "happy," "sad," "mad," and "surprised."

**Help the bee find its way.** Distribute copies of page 56. Identify the beginning sounds and letters of objects on the page. Ask children to match the bees to the correct objects.

## Day 2

**Reread the poem** using one of the suggested methods from Day 1. Brainstorm and list words that rhyme with grow and row. Add them to the word bank.

**How tall are you?** Ask students if plants are alive. List living things and decide what they all have in common; living things grow. After a simple measurement lesson with the class, measure each child. Prepare a few sunflower stencils. Have students color and cut out sunflower shapes. Put student names and heights in the center of the flowers. Then cut strips of construction paper for the stems and attach them to the flowers so that together they measure the correct height of each student. Display these on a wall or bulletin board labeled "We Are Growing."

**Read and discuss** *A Tree is Nice* by Janice Udry (Harper, 1987). Make a list of the many wonderful ways trees enhance our lives. Cut a tree trunk and branches from butcher paper. Add leaves. On them, write student suggestions about "why trees are nice." Remind children that trees are our largest plants. Talk about ways to take care of the earth's plant life.

# Sample Lessons for "Mary, Mary, Quite Contrary" (cont.)

## Day 3

**Assemble and color the Little Book** (pages 59-61). Read the poem together using the Little Books.

**Find out where plants come from** and what they need for growth. Display various seeds and bulbs. Plant seeds at the science center and keep a chart for daily care. (Give each student a container, soil, and seeds. They may bring these home when plants are established.)

**Practice 'm' words** at centers, using the phonics activity on page 58 as a clothespin game. Make word rings with children and encourage them to add more 'm' words throughout the unit.

**Sort living things** into plant and animal categories. Have students cut out pictures of plants and animals from magazines. Glue them onto non-woven interfacing squares and label each with its plant or animal name. Divide a flannel board into two sections (plant/animal) and ask students to sort the pictures by category.

## Day 4

**Reread the poem chorally.** Replace the flowers in the poem with other flowers or objects, and recite the poem with the new words. As an alternative, display the poem on the overhead (use Little Book transparencies). Cover selected words (cloze method) and ask children to identify the missing words. Have children practice the poem at a center using flannel board patterns from pages 54-55.

**Watch Mary's flower grow.** Assemble the flower on page 57. Children may bring these home and recite the poem while making the flower grow.

**Build a garden** in the block center. Use blocks to fence in the garden. Children can make flowers from egg carton cups, painted and attached to pipe cleaner stems. Cut leaves from green construction paper, punch holes at the bottom, and pull stems through each. Put the flowers in decorated milk cartons. If desired, add play fruits and vegetables to the garden.

# Patterns

See pages 52-53 for suggested activities.

# Patterns (cont.)

See pages 52-53 for suggested activities.

*Mary, Mary, Quite Contrary*

# Matching Letters in Mary's Garden

**Directions:** Cut out the bee ovals. Match the beginning letter on the bee to the beginning letter of the object. Glue the bee on the correct X.

# Watch Mary's Flower Grow

**Directions:** Color and cut out the flower. Then cut around the outside border of the picture of Mary and along the dotted slit inside. Pull the bottom of the flower down through the slit (fold flaps in first). Slowly move the flower up to make it grow.

slit

fold

fold

# Phonics Activity

See page 53 for suggested activity.

# Little Book

My Little Book of

# "Mary, Mary, Quite Contrary"

Name _____

## Mary, Mary, quite contrary,

1

# Little Book (cont.)

## How does your garden grow?

2

## With silver bells and cockle shells,

3

# Little Book *(cont.)*

## And pretty maids all in a row.

4

## The End

5

# Sample Lessons for "Little Miss Muffet"

## Getting Ready

Set up a bulletin board entitled "Am I a spider or an insect?" Make a yarn web as background. Write the following riddles on chart paper and place in the center of the bulletin board:

*I have 6 legs*
*And very strange eyes.*
*I crawl and sting,*
*Hop, fly, and chew.*
*Better watch out!*
*I might sting you.*
*What am I?* **(insect)**

*I have 8 legs,*
*And sometimes 8 eyes.*
*I sit in a web,*
*And wait for flies.*
*What am I?* **(spider)**

Surround the riddles with pictures and labels of insects and spiders. Use as an interactive bulletin board by having students match pictures and labels or sort insects and spiders. Create and display a word bank web using yarn and butcher paper. Attach words to it. Add spider, insect, and plant books to a reading center. Prepare flannel board patterns (pages 65-67 ) and nonwoven interfacing word cards for the poem.

Set up a screen wire bug house or a bug center in which insects and spiders may be collected and observed. (Remind children not to touch creatures, as some are poisonous.)

## Day 1

**Read "Little Miss Muffet"** after introducing insects and spiders. If both have been collected, have the class observe the movement and characteristics of insects and spiders. Ask how they feel about insects and spiders. As an alternative, use the bulletin board display to introduce the poem. Point out that spiders are arachnids. Read "Little Miss Muffet" using the flannel board patterns on pages 65-66 and Little Book pages 70-72. Discuss the following questions: What frightened Miss Muffet? Are you frightened by insects or spiders? Would you have done what Miss Muffet did?

**Compare and sort** arachnids and insects using the bulletin board and patterns. Discuss the differences between the two groups.

**Create spider webs.** Read *The Very Busy Spider* by Eric Carle (Putnam, 1984). Call students' attention to the process of building the web. Let them feel its texture. Then let students make webs following these directions. Fold 9" x 12" pieces of black or dark blue construction paper in half lengthwise, widthwise, and diagonally. Open and trace over fold lines with white crayon. Starting at the center, add a crayon spiral over the criss-crossed lines. Glue on spiders from pattern pages. Variations: For more textures "trace" over lines with white glue or puffy paints, or dip pieces of string in thinned white glue and lay on paper. Let dry thoroughly before moving and gluing on spiders.

# Sample Lessons for "Little Miss Muffet" *(cont.)*

## Day 2

**Reread the poem while children dramatize the actions.** Have a child sit on a large pillow or stool eating from a bowl while another child dangles a play spider.

**Write a story sequel to the poem.** Ask students where Miss Muffet might have gone. Copy the students' responses into a story chart and display them along with illustrations of Miss Muffet's adventure.

**Pretend to be spiders.** Have children walk like spiders and pretend to build a web. Have them act out catching an insect and walking on the web in rain, wind, snow, etc.

**Practice 'Ll'** using the phonics activity on page 69 as a clothespin game. First, label 'l' words in the room. Have children bring in 'l' words clipped from magazines and newspapers. Glue them to construction paper. Label each with the student's name and "My 'l' words." Encourage children to share a toy or object that begins with 'l.'

## Day 3

**Reread the poem** using Little Book transparencies. Distribute Little Book pages 70-72 and have students color and assemble them to share at home.

**Learn about life cycles.** Ask children how they think insects and spiders grow (stages). Read *The Very Hungry Caterpillar* by Eric Carle (Putnam, 1981). Prepare sets of life cycle cards from page 68 using index paper. Laminate and cut along dashed lines. After discussing the life cycle of butterflies and spiders, have students sequence the cards at a center. (Provide an answer key.) Compare the growth stages of insects and arachnids.

**Practice counting.** Duplicate the insect and spider patterns (page 65 and 67). Ask children to count how many legs a given number of spiders or insects have altogether.

## Day 4

**Reread "Little Miss Muffet."** Ask children if they were once afraid of something that no longer frightens them. Talk about overcoming fears. Then add the following verse to the poem and discuss what it might mean:

> *But as she got older,*
> *Miss Muffet grew bolder,*
> *Until one fine, sunny spring day.*
> *Our Little Miss Muffet,*
> *Went back to her tuffet,*
> *And there she decided to stay.*

Have children dramatize the entire poem. This may be done in small groups with stick puppets.

# Sample Lessons for "Little Miss Muffet" *(cont.)*

**Sing and pantomime** "The Eency Weency Spider" (*Tom Glazer's Treasury of Songs for Children* by Tom Glazer; Doubleday, 1964).

**Play "Spider, Spider. Who's got the spider?"** Have one child sit, with eyes closed, in the center of a circle of children. Another child hides the spider (a toy spider or eraser) behind a student. The child in the center tries to guess who has the spider. Allow children to give clues.

**Make a tasty cheese-noodle dish.** Curd, the coagulated part of soured milk, is used in the making of cheese. The watery part that separates from curd is the whey. A good way to demonstrate whey is to show the watery separation on the top of a carton of yogurt that has been sitting for a while. Explain to children that the curds and whey Little Miss Muffet was eating is similar to cottage cheese. Prepare and enjoy the following noodle dish in class.

*Recipe*

### Cheesy Noodles

Cook and drain an 8 ounce (225 g) package of egg noodles. Mix the noodles with 2 cups ($\frac{1}{2}$ L) of sour cream, 1 $\frac{1}{2}$ cups (375 mL) of cottage cheese, 1 teaspoon (5 mL) of salt and 1 $\frac{1}{2}$ teaspoons (7 mL) of chopped parsley. Place into a greased casserole dish, top with pats of butter, and bake for 30 minutes in a 350 degrees Fahrenheit (190 degrees Celsius) oven.

When done, top with $\frac{1}{2}$ cup (125 mL) of grated cheddar cheese, 2 tablespoons (30 mL) of butter or margarine, and a little paprika. Place in oven until cheese topping melts.

As an alternative, children could have a simple cottage cheese snack, such as cottage cheese and wedges of fruit.

**Write a Big Book** using student dictated story ideas. Reread *The Very Busy Spider* by Eric Carle (Putnam, 1989). Have children choose other animals that may have conversed with the spider, and write down their responses on Big Book pages. Children can then illustrate the text. You may wish to create a different spider adventure instead, using *The Very Busy Spider* as a story starter. Or, write an innovation, using a very hungry ant or busy bee as the main character.

64

# Patterns

See pages 62-63 for suggested activities.

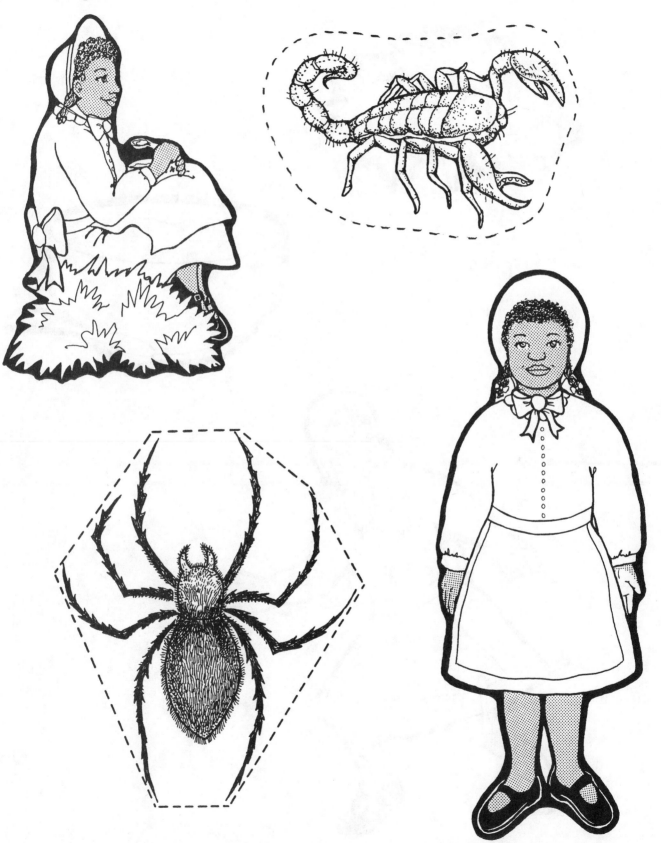

# Patterns *(cont.)*

See pages 62-63 for suggested activities.

# Patterns (cont.)

See pages 62-63 for suggested activities.

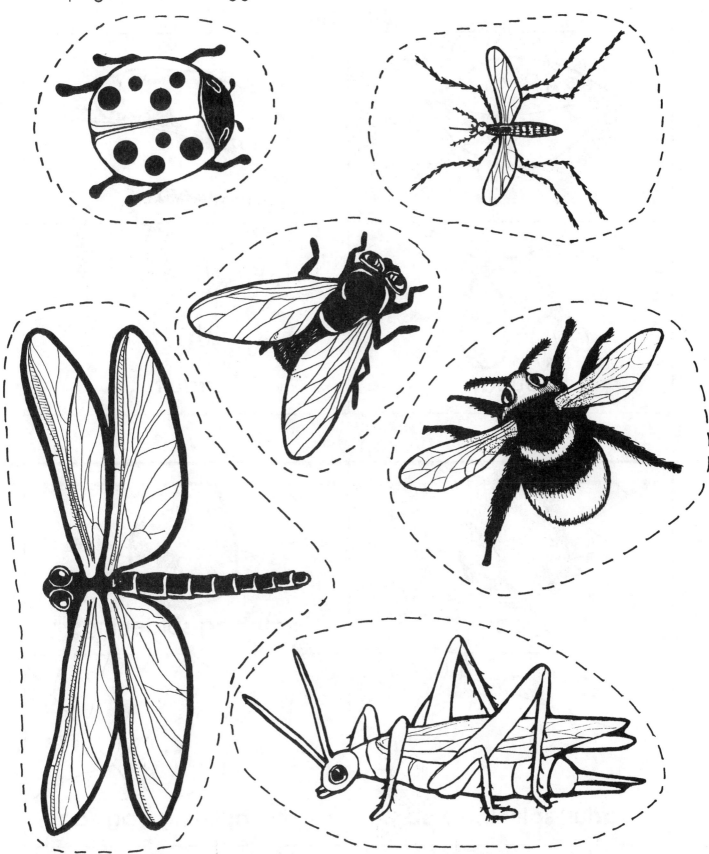

# Life Cycle Cards

See page 63 for suggested activity.

## Butterfly

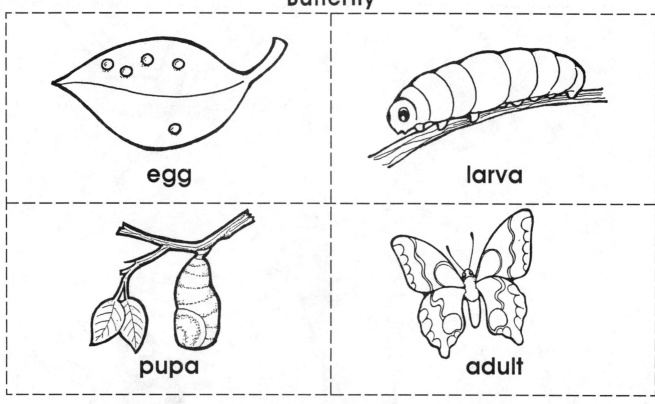

egg

larva

pupa

adult

## Spider

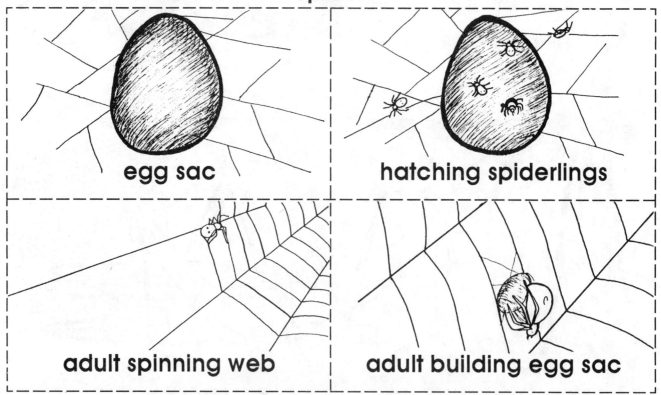

egg sac

hatching spiderlings

adult spinning web

adult building egg sac

# Phonics Activity

See page 63 for suggested activities.

# Little Book

- - - - - - - - - - - - - - - - - - - - - - - - - - - - - - - - - - - - - - - - - -

## My Little Book of
## "Little Miss Muffet"

Name _____

- - - - - - - - - - - - - - - - - - - - - - - - - - - - - - - - - - - - - - - - - -

## Little Miss Muffet
## Sat on a tuffet,

1

- - - - - - - - - - - - - - - - - - - - - - - - - - - - - - - - - - - - - - - - - -

# Little Book (cont.)

## Eating her curds and whey;

2

## Along came a spider,

3

# Little Book (cont.)

## Who sat down beside her,

4

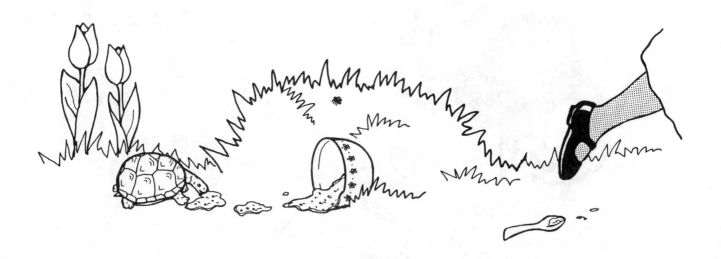

## And frightened Miss Muffet away.

5

72

# Sample Lessons for "Jack and Jill"

## Getting Ready

Stock the science center with a few pails, measuring cups, water, and various kinds of containers for holding water. Add books about play safety, the water cycle, conservation, and related nursery rhymes, such as "Jack Be Nimble" and "Little Jack Horner." Make a Word Bank Well. Using butcher paper, draw and cut out a large well and pail. Display these on a wall or bulletin board. Add words to the well throughout the unit. Put the poem title, or the entire poem (see Little Book pages 79-81 for text), on the pail and "hang" it from the top of the well. Students can make and cut out flowers to add to the base of the well.

## Day 1

**Introduce the poem.** Use the science center materials and the Word Bank Well to spark discussion about "Jack and Jill." Read the poem from an overhead transparency, using the flannel board patterns on page 75, or from the well wall chart. Discuss the following questions: Why were Jack and Jill getting water? What do you think caused Jack to fall? Why do you think Jill came tumbling after? Where were they going to get the water? What do you think the words *fetch*, *crown* and *tumble* mean?

**Identify opposites.** Introduce the word "opposites." Have one child come up and be Jack and another, Jill. Ask how the children are different. Explain that "boy" and "girl" are opposites. Use the poem to find the opposites "up" and "down." Read "Jack Be Nimble" and ask what the opposite of "over the candlestick" would be. Teach the students the following fingerplay to illustrate "in" and "out":

*Jack-in-the-box*

*Sits so still.* (*Hide thumb in fist.*)

*Won't you come out?*

*Yes, I will!* (*Thumb pops out.*)

**Make a Big Book about safety.** Ask children if they think Jack or Jill were hurt when they fell. Discuss safety rules when playing, riding bikes, running, etc. Create a Big Book entitled "We Need To Be Safe When We..." Copy each student's response ("ride our bikes," for example) onto a page. Have students illustrate these.

# Sample Lessons for "Jack and Jill" (cont.)

## Day 2

**Reread "Jack and Jill" together several times.** Clap or tap the rhythm. Find the rhyming words, write them in the word bank, and add others. Add movement by having children bounce balls to the rhythm of the poem.

**Learn more about opposites.** Use other stories and rhymes to teach opposites. For example, "Pease, Porridge, Hot" can be used to teach "hot" and "cold." *The Tortoise and the Hare* could be used as an example of "fast" and "slow." *Push, Pull, Empty, Full: A Book of Opposites* by Tana Hoban (Macmillan, 1972) is an excellent book for learning opposites. Copy pages 76 and 77 onto tag or index paper. Discuss the pictures and labels on the pages. (You may want to practice matching words on the overhead with the children first.) Laminate and cut into cards, or glue to felt to make a flannel board game. Make enough copies so that children can play "Memory" or "Concentration" in pairs.

**Learn about water.** At the science center melt ice in cups. Ask children to guess what will happen and how high the water level will be. As an extension, boil water and discuss what happens to the liquid.

## Day 3

**Read and then sing** "Jack and Jill." Add movement to the song.

**Estimate and then count** how many cups it takes to fill a pail of water. Use equipment from the science center. Children may work in supervised groups. Discuss each group's results.

**Do "Jack and Jill" physical education activities.** Practice tumbling on mats or grass. Run relays up and down a small hill. Have a water relay. (Children walk quickly back and forth carrying a large spoon or small cup of water.)

**Learn more words that begin with 'j.'** Start with jumping jacks and jogging in place and remind children that both these exercise names begin with 'j.' Find and list other 'j' words, including student names. Use phonics activity on page 78. Have students place a marker on 'j' words or color the pictures that represent 'j' words.

## Day 4

**Reread the poem using flannel board patterns** from page 75. Write an innovation with the class, changing the characters, where they went, and what happened. For example, Jane and Joe could go to the shore and get splashed and tossed about by a wave.

**Make little books.** Distribute pages 79-81, color and cut out the pages. Recite the poem together as the children follow along in the little books.

**Use water colors to paint a scene.** Draw large outlines of a well, Jack and Jill, a hill, pail, etc., on butcher paper. Have students paint inside the outlines. Label the objects.

# Patterns

See pages 73-74 for suggested activities.

*Jack and Jill*

# Patterns for Opposites

See page 74 for directions.

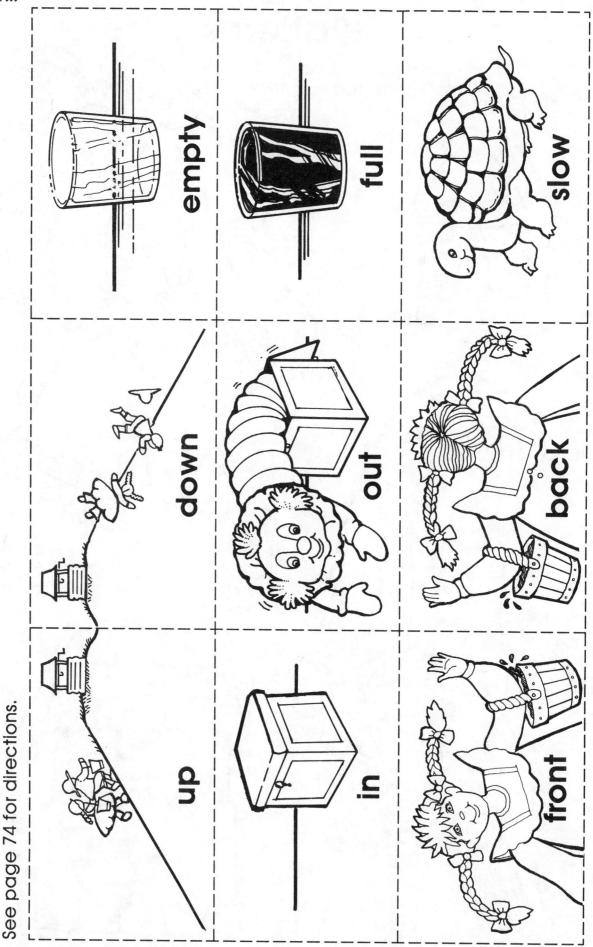

empty

full

slow

down

out

back

up

in

front

# Patterns for Opposites *(cont.)*

See page 74 for directions.

big

little

fast

few

night

cold

many

day

hot

*Jack and Jill*

# Phonics Activity

See page 74 for suggested activity.

# Little Book

## My Little Book of
## "Jack and Jill"

Name _____

## Jack and Jill went up the hill,

1

# Little Book (cont.)

## To fetch a pail of water;

2

## Jack fell down and broke his crown,

3

# Little Book *(cont.)*

## And Jill came tumbling after.

4

## The End

5

# Sample Lessons for
# "Little Boy Blue" & "Little Bo-Peep"

## Getting Ready

Prepare the Little Boy Blue pattern from page 84 in a variety of felt colors. If possible, plan a visit to a feed store or farm. Add farm animal books to the reading center. Set up a word bank for 'b' words using a large drawing of a horn, with words "blowing out" of it. Cut word ring cards for students to use during the unit. Assemble a file of both domestic and wild animal pictures.

## Day 1

**Introduce the "Little Boy Blue" nursery rhyme.** See Little Book pages 88-89 for text. Display a horn, toy sheep, cow, and flannel board patterns (pages 84-85). After reading the poem, ask the following questions: Why would Little Boy Blue blow his horn? What do you think tending the sheep means? Was Little Boy Blue being responsible? (Talk about responsibilities and chores. Relate this to classroom jobs or home chores.)

**Classify domestic and wild animals.** Talk about domesticated animals and what characteristics make them different from wild animals. Cut out pictures of each group and back them with felt. Divide a flannel board in half with yarn and label sections "tame" and "wild." Place in a center for students to use for classification.

**Animal Three-in-a-Row.** Make a gameboard for each student by dividing 9" x 12" construction or index paper into 9 squares (like a tic-tac-toe board). Duplicate two sets of animal pictures from page 86 onto index paper and cut out the animal cards. Glue 9 assorted cards on each gameboard. (Mix these so that no gameboards are alike. You may use two or more of the same animal on a gameboard.) The rest of the animal cards become the deck from which to call out animals. The teacher or a student caller picks a card from the deck and announces its name. The deck is reshuffled for continued use. Have children put markers (buttons, pebbles, seeds, etc.) on the gameboard if they have the announced animal. The first student with three in a row (horizontally, vertically, or diagonally) wins.

## Day 2

**Introduce "Little Bo-Peep."** Read the poem from a chart or Little Book transparencies (pages 90-91). Compare the poem to "Little Boy Blue," noting similarities and differences. Ask the following questions: How do you suppose Little Bo-Peep lost her sheep? Do you think they came home? What would you do if you got lost?

**Shuck corn.** Bring in ears (or whole stalks, if possible) of sweet corn. Discuss the parts of the corn plant and have students remove the husk from the corn. Identify kernels and cob. Cook and enjoy corn on the cob. Have children compare the kernels of corn before and after cooking.

# Sample Lessons for
# "Little Boy Blue" & "Little Bo-Peep"

## *(cont.)*

**Practice counting.** Present the following situation to the class: Little Boy Blue lived next door to Little Bo-Peep, who was always losing her sheep. She came crying to him one day. "Little Boy Blue, I'm supposed to have 6 sheep. I can't tell if I found all of them. Could you help me?" Put 5 sheep on the flannel board or overhead projector and ask children to discover if sheep are missing. Try several problems, using different numbers.

**Learn the names of baby animals.** Refer to sheep and cows from the poems. Talk about lambs and calves and other baby animals. Display pictures of adult and baby animals and label them. Put these in the science center.

## Day 3

**Reread "Little Boy Blue" and "Little Bo-Peep"** from Little Book transparencies. Have children act out each using flannel board patterns from pages 84 and 85.

**Make a class Lost and Found Book.** Remind children that in each poem, the animals might have gotten lost. Ask them if they ever lost something. Have students respond to the following sentences and record the statements into an illustrated class book:

*I lost a (what). I found it (where, when, or how).*

**Cut out, color, and assemble Little Books.** Use pages 88-91 to make Little Books of "Little Boy Blue" and "Little Bo-Peep." Read and sing them when done.

**Practice phonics.** Find and say the 'b' words in each poem. Label the 'b' words in the room. Add student names that begin with 'b' to the Word Bank. Make copies of phonics page 87 and use it as a clothespin game at a center.

## Day 4

**Reread "Little Boy Blue" using the following color game.** Copy the Little Boy Blue pattern onto a variety of felt colors. Use yellow felt for his horn. Place all the felt boys on the flannel board and hide the horn behind one of them. Ask children to guess which boy has the horn by reciting the poem using a color to replace the word blue. The child who guesses the correct color may hide the horn for the next game.

**Sing and add movement to related poems.** Discuss the similarities between "Baa, Baa Black Sheep," "Mary Had a Little Lamb," and the poems in this unit. Sing each and add appropriate movements to show the action in each.

**Make corn bread or popcorn.** Use your favorite corn bread recipe to make and enjoy in class. On another day enjoy a popcorn treat.

# Patterns

See pages 82-83 for suggested activities.

# Patterns *(cont.)*

See pages 82-83 for suggested activities.

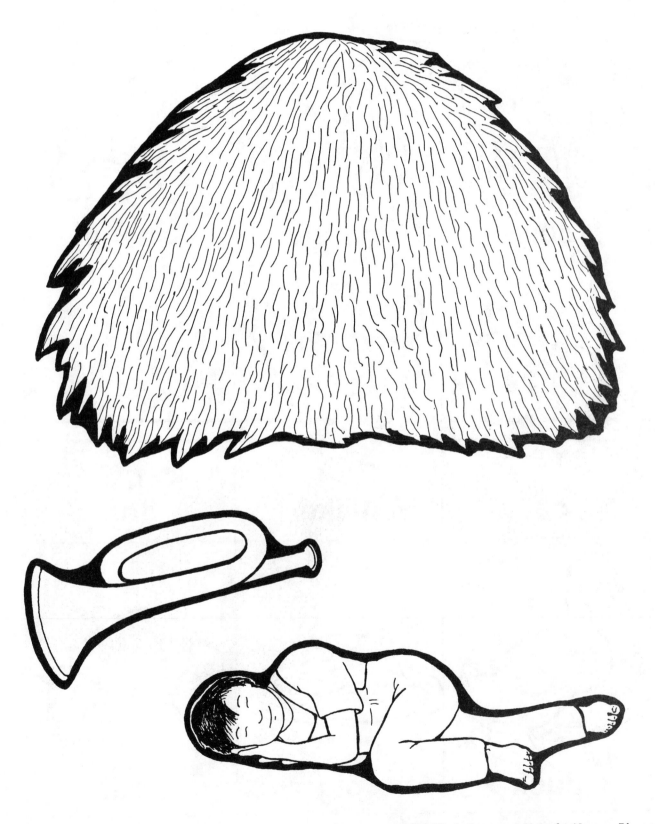

# Animal Three-in-a-Row

See page 82 for directions.

cow

horse

sheep

cat

chicken

dog

duck

pig

turtle

# Phonics Activity

See directions on page 83.

# Little Book (cont.)

## My Little Book of
# "Little Boy Blue"

Name _____

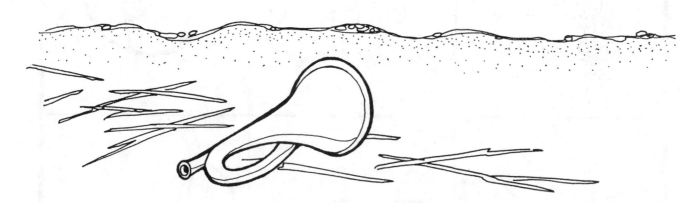

## Little Boy Blue,
## Come blow your horn,

1

# Little Book *(cont.)*

**The sheep's in the meadow,**
**The cow's in the corn.**

2

**Where is the boy**
**who looks after the sheep?**

**He's under the haystack, fast asleep.**

3

# Little Book (cont.)

## My Little Book of
## "Little Bo-Peep"

Name _____

## Little Bo-Peep has lost her sheep,

1

# Little Book *(cont.)*

## And doesn't know where to find them;

2

## Leave them alone, and they'll come home,
## Wagging their tails behind them.

3

# Sample Lessons for "Twinkle, Twinkle, Little Star"

## Getting Ready

Set up a "Starry Night" bulletin board. Create a black butcher paper background and have children make chalk or white art pencil stars using star stencils. Fill the sky with stars. Make a dark blue or gray ground area and attach figures of children gazing upward. Write the poem on large chart paper and place it in the center of the bulletin board. See Little Book pages 99-101 for text. As an alternative, cut out yellow stars, write children's names or 's' words on them, and place them in constellation clusters on the bulletin board. (Connect each star of a constellation to the others with yarn.) Display a Word Bank using a large star background, or a shuttle or rocket ship silhouette. If possible, arrange a visit to a planetarium. Be sure to update the reading center with books on stars, outer space, and the solar system.

## Day 1

**Introduce the poem.** Show a large star shape and ask students to identify it and where they may have seen stars or star-shaped objects. Use the bulletin board and pictures to focus student attention on the unit theme. Read "Twinkle, Twinkle, Little Star" using the bulletin board poem. Ask the following questions: How many stars do you think there are in the sky? What else is in the sky? What is a diamond (draw shape)? How do we travel to the moon today? Talk about astronauts. Discuss "far" and "near" and make a student-generated list of things that are close to us and far away.

**Share a global experience.** Begin by showing a globe and teaching simple map skills. Help children understand that all people live on earth. Students can make an earth from a piece of blue construction paper by tracing around coffee can lids and cutting out the circle patterns. Make land by drawing and coloring free form shapes. Read *What the Moon Is Like* by Franklyn M. Branley (Harper, 1986). Suggest that children build a moon city in the block center. Build a lunar rover using interlocking plastic blocks.

**Write similes.** Hold up several objects and ask children to describe them by comparing each to another object. For example, an orange is like a ball. Use the poem simile, "like a diamond in the sky," and ask to what it refers. Make sentence strips using statements such as "The moon is like a . . .", "The sun is like a . . .", etc. Ask students to fill in the blanks with suggestions. Write and illustrate student responses in a class big book, or display individual pages around the room.

**Discuss space travel.** Display shuttle, land rover, and other space-related pictures and use the flannel board patterns (pages 94-95) to inspire student ideas about outer space. Refer to the bulletin board to talk about constellations. Make dots on construction paper to simulate constellations. Poke holes where the dots are, and shine a light source through the holes (darken the room). Observe the stars on the ceiling!

# Sample Lessons for "Twinkle, Twinkle, Little Star" *(cont.)*

## Day 2

**Reread the poem** using a transparency of the Little Book on pages 99-101. Use a cloze technique by covering words and asking children to name the missing word. Display the following poem and have students say words that could complete the poem:

> *Sparkle, sparkle, little stream,*
> *You are _____er  than you seem.*
> *On your banks we like to play,*
> *Having fun throughout the day.*

**Make a "Super Star" Board.** Prepare a grid on large butcher paper with squares in which each student can display photos, awards, memorabilia, etc. Have children display and share their "treasures" with the class. Surround the board with star shapes.

**Practice 's' words.** Make a list of 's' words from the unit. Have students cut out 6" stars. Hang them from the ceiling with an 's' word on one side and a picture on the other. Do phonics page 98, using stars or other markers on pictures beginning with 's.' Match pictures and words on page 97.

## Day 3

**Read another star poem, "Star Light, Star Bright."** Discuss wishes. Make and illustrate a class book of student-dictated wishes. Or, make and display a class wish list.

**How many stars does our flag have?** Distribute copies of page 96. Count the number of stars and color the flag as it should look.

**Practice set counting.** Using index paper, make copies of the pentagram from page 95. Have students number the points from 1-5. Practice counting how many points there are in 2 stars, 3 stars, etc.

## Day 4

**Reread and sing the poem.** Assemble and color the Little Books (pages 99-101). Have students recite or sing the poem together.

**What is a diamond shape?** Display a large diamond shape and ask children what objects have the same shape. List responses. Make and color diamond shapes, or cut out different colored diamonds from construction paper and glue them onto butcher paper to make a class mosaic. Diamond shapes could also be strung on necklaces by punching holes in one end and attaching them to yarn. Write 's' words on each diamond.

**Play "Moon, Moon, Star"** following "Duck, Duck, Goose" rules.

# Patterns

See pages 92-93 for suggested activities.

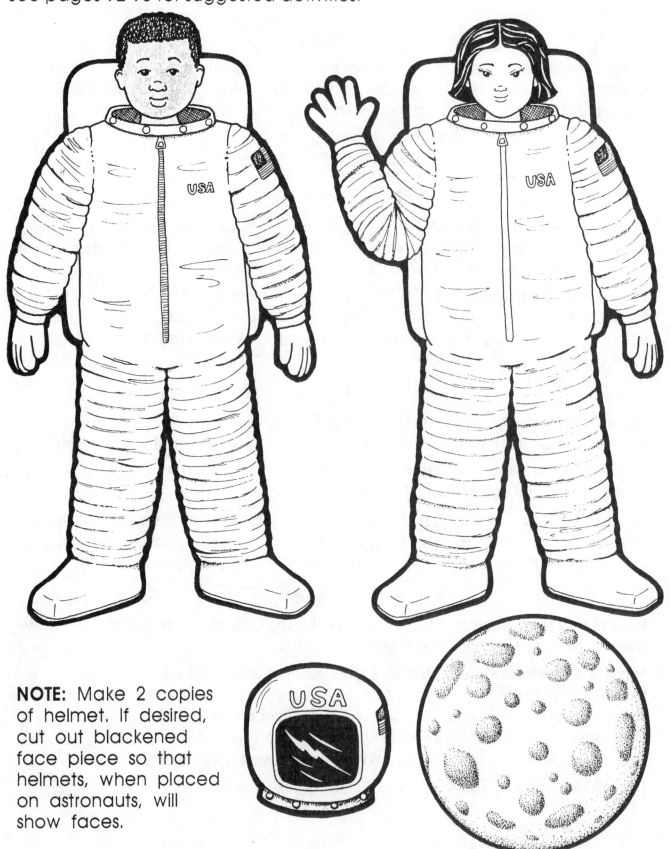

**NOTE:** Make 2 copies of helmet. If desired, cut out blackened face piece so that helmets, when placed on astronauts, will show faces.

# Patterns *(cont.)*

See pages 92-93 for suggested activities.

Name _____

# United States Flag

See page 93 for activity.

Name _____

# Word Match

**Directions:** Color each picture. Then cut the pictures along the dashed lines. Glue each picture in the box next to its name.

| | | |
|---|---|---|
| **sun** | | |
| **star** | | |
| **world** | | |
| **moon** | | |
| **sky** | | |

# Phonics Activity

See page 93 for directions.

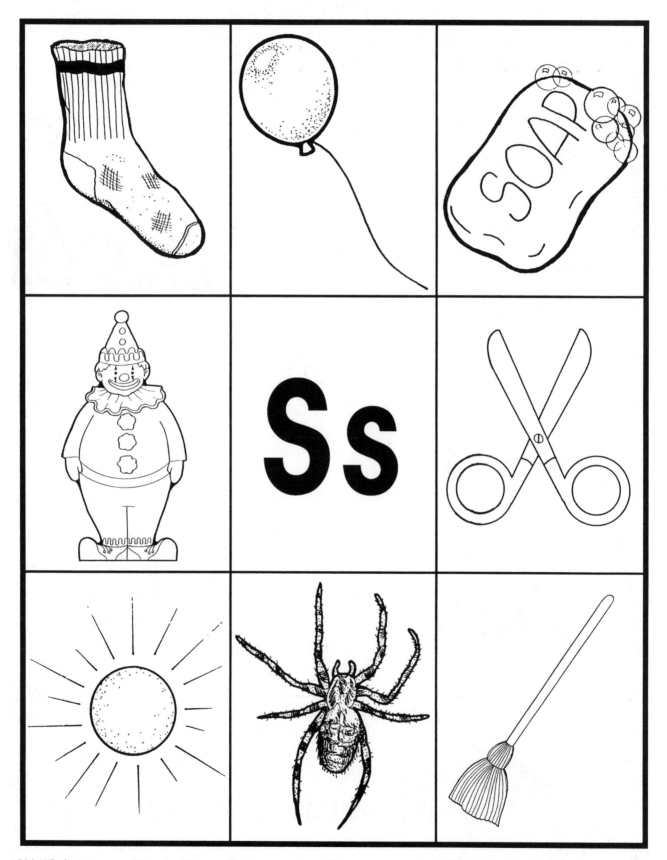

# Little Book

My Little Book of

# "Twinkle, Twinkle, Little Star"

Name _____

## Twinkle, twinkle, little star,

1

# Little Book (cont.)

## How I wonder what you are!

2

## Up above the world so high,

3

# Little Book *(cont.)*

## Like a diamond in the sky.

4

## The End

5

# Sample Lessons for "There Was an Old Woman"

## Getting Ready

Display books about shoes, shoe making, unusual houses, etc., in the reading center. Start a Word Bank by making a large shoe shape with a 'w' in the center. Have little shoes with 'w' words surrounding it. Underline or circle the beginning letter. Plan a visit to a nearby shoe repair or shoemaker's shop. Make a chart of the nursery rhyme. See text on the Little Book pages 110-112.

## Day 1

**Prepare a bulletin board** with a large shoe house in the center and figures of children playing outside around the shoe. Display and read the poem. Children may notice the difference between last lines of the Little Book version (page 112) and the traditional verse. Discuss the meaning of each and decide why they think the change was made. Ask the following questions: Do you think it was too crowded in the shoe? How many children do you think lived in the shoe? Do you think this was a problem for the old woman? Why? What does a shoemaker do? Have you ever been to a shoe repair shop? What is done there? List different kinds of shoes and their uses. (Have pictures of types of footwear available.) Discuss materials used in making shoes.

**Write a bulletin board story.** Ask children if they would like to live in a shoe house. Write student responses on sentence strips (I would or wouldn't like to live in a shoe house because...) and attach these next to the figures of the children on the bulletin board. (Add student names to the figures and/or sentences.)

**Help the old woman find her children.** Distribute copies of page 108 and ask children to find the correct path through the maze.

## Day 2

**Reread the poem** using the flannel board patterns from pages 104-105. Review unusual houses as in "Peter, Peter, Pumpkin Eater" and "There was a Crooked Man." Build shoe houses or crooked houses in the block center.

**Have a shoe hunt.** Ask children to place one of their shoes in a class pile of shoes. At a given signal, students dash to find their shoes, put them back on, and quickly sit down.

**Find 'w' words.** Locate and label objects that begin with 'w' and write student words in the Word Bank. Make word rings with the children. Place copies of the phonics activity on page 109 in a center to be used as a clothespin game.

# Sample Lessons for "There Was an Old Woman" *(cont.)*

## Day 3

**Present "The Further Adventures of the Old Woman Who Lived in a Shoe,"** using the flannel board patterns on pages 104-105. Reproduce and read the story on page 106 to the children, using the flannel board characters from this and other units. Encourage children to add new verses.

**Make a Big Book.** Tell the children to imagine that the old woman is coming to their school to ask them where her children are. On each page, write "She asked (student name), 'Have you seen my children?' But (student name) was (doing her math, reading a book, etc.)" Have each child contribute a sentence page. At the end of the book, the old woman finds her children in the library.

**To whom is the Old Woman talking?** Review the letters 'p,' 'b,' 'h,' 'm,' and 'j.' Using page 107, have students match the letter in the box to the picture whose name begins with that letter. Draw a line from the letter box to the correct picture.

She asked Lauren, "Have you seen my children?" But Lauren was reading a book.

She asked Jessica, "Have you seen my children?" But Jessica was doing her math.

## Day 4

**Reread the first two lines of "There Was an Old Woman" together.** Add "There was..." and ask each child to call out his/her name. Finish with the sentence, "How will these children all fit in the shoe?"

**Make and color the Little Book pages** 110-112 and share the story at home.

**Reinforce counting.** Use the "One potato, two potato" counting rhythm in the following poem:

> *One shoe, two shoes, three shoes, four;*
> *Five shoes, six shoes, seven shoes more.*
> *Eight shoes, nine shoes, ten shoes, eleven;*
> *Now start all over and count to seven.*
>
> (Student counts to seven and chooses another child to say the poem.)

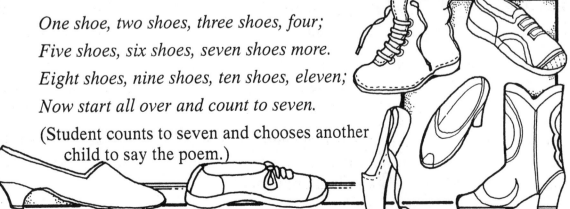

# Patterns

See pages 102-103 for suggested activities.

# Patterns *(cont.)*

See pages 102-103 for suggested activities.

# The Further Adventures of the Old Woman Who Lived in a Shoe

*When the old woman woke up, her children were gone.*

*No children in the bedroom.*

*No children in the kitchen.*

*No children in the yard.*

*She went to look for them.*

*She met Jack and Jill.*

*"Have you seen my children?" she asked.*

*But Jack and Jill were crying.*

*She met Little Miss Muffet.*

*"Have you seen my children?" she asked.*

*But Little Miss Muffet ran away.*

*She met Little Boy Blue.*

*"Have you seen my children?" she asked.*

*But Little Boy Blue was asleep.*

*She met Mary, Mary, Quite Contrary.*

*"Have you seen my children?" she asked.*

*But Mary was busy watering her garden.*

*So the old woman went to school.*

*"Have you seen my children?" she asked.*

*"Yes," said the teacher. "They are in the library."*

*What good children!*

# The Old Woman is talking to . . .

See page 103 for directions.

Jack and Jill

Mary

Peter

Humpty Dumpty

Little Boy Blue

b

h

m

p

j

# Help the Old Woman
# Find Her Children

**Directions:** Using your finger or a crayon, trace the one correct path that leads the old woman to the schoolhouse and her children.

# Phonics Activity

See page 102 for directions.

# Little Book

My Little Book of

# "There Was an Old Woman"

Name _____

## There was an old woman
## who lived in a shoe,

1

# Little Book (cont.)

## She had so many children she didn't know what to do;

2

## She gave them some broth without any bread;

3

# Little Book (cont.)

## She hugged them all fondly and put them to bed.

4

## The End

5